Complications of the Heart

Complications of the Heart

—**Winner, 2002 Robert Phillips Poetry Chapbook Prize**—

Texas Review Press
Huntsville, Texas

FIRST EDITION, 2003

Requests for permission to reproduce material from this work should be sent to:

Permissions
Texas Review Press
Box 2146
English Department
Sam Houston State University
Huntsville, TX 77341-2146

Acknowledgments:

The Bridge, Cimarron Review, ForPoetry.com, Journal of the American Medical Association (JAMA), The Ledge, The Literary Review, The Lyric, Passages North, Poet Lore, Poetry, Prairie Schooner, Shenandoah, Skylark, Southern Humanities Review, The Texas Review

The author would like to thank Peter Brown for his love and encouragement, and Jeffrey Levine for patiently working his editorial magic on early drafts of these poems.

Cover design by Paul Ruffin

Cover photograph by Larry Kellogg

Library of Congress Cataloging-in-Publication Data

Carlson, Nancy Naomi, 1949-
    Complications of the heart / Nancy Naomi Carlson.— 1st ed.
        p. cm.
    ISBN 1-881515-56-7 (alk. paper)
    I. Title.
    PS3553.A7327 C37 2003
    811'.54—dc21
                                                        2003002456

For my Mother and Father
and for Seth & Rachel,
with love

Table of Contents

Touch-Me-Not

How to placate our past loves who beg
to be let in like the dead?
Lie down with them and they demand
a bigger space than the foot of the bed—
like jewelweed they run wild and reseed

themselves at the slightest touch.
Like fungi they compete for the air you need.
Throw them the dried bone of desire, and see
them scatter like droplets from the sea
after extra freight is pitched

overboard, but know they can rise again
in one great wave to pull you under, down
to the splash of color and show—
the sea anemone's lure below.

Selle De La Veau A La Tosca

Picture braised, sliced veal loins purloined
from the bone and restored, laid over a bed
of cut pasta with truffles and cream—

did I mention the sauce Mornay?—for queen
or diva a fitting tribute, or the perfect dish
for the prelude to a tryst set, let's say,

in Rome against the ruins, or Palazzo Farnese,
or maybe the Tiber, sweat beading on our sunburned
flesh like rain on an apple, golden and delicious, rare

and forbidden, each bite's aftertaste
another hunger, a scene glazed like raku, hot
from the kiln—cerulean sky, white crests of a river

out of control, an overflow, an other-worldly tint—
Sant'Andrea della Valle bells tolling, veristic pitch.

Sari-Covered Nights

I'm a brass-bellied Buddha's dream,
an evening of gauze, stars blue
and windswept, the quicksilver moon
tangled in the limbs of a lone banyan tree.
Oh rub me to a blinding sheen!

I am the sitar's ragged throat, pitched
between here and when,
caught in quarter tones, worlds bewitched.
Why these four arms so long unkissed?
Am I not your goddess?

My five mouths roll their uvulas,
guttural as high winds crossing desert dunes.
Is there not a stopping place for us,
adrift, two souls who speak in tongues?

What Cannot Be Held

I might have called her *Chayala* for life,
but knew her only as shadow and light,

an echo on a sonogram screen,
a preview of a chord I'd never hear.

Her image was gathered from swipes of a probe.
Sifting through layers of tissue and bone,

the trained eye could pick out from fluid's play
the outline of heart and head, digits that waved

like sea anemones. Different views—
cross-sectional maps—guided the search for clues

to the flaw, knitted in code and handed down
the line. Figure rose from changing ground,

hovered ghostlike and then, reversing roles,
broke up into static that would not hold.

The Page Turner

Second-hand thrill, and I ride the music's edge:
dog-eared score measured for piano and strings,

this Penaforte trio unfolds like a rose,
minor chords' perfume to fade at the end.

The pianist depends on my sleight of hand turns
to preserve the unbroken line, even

as a hand-pressed seam; my slip could mean
a missed half step in a trill, or worse—

the airborne page drifting out of range,
so even those in the dark could catch a mistake.

I stay fixed on the staves—an effusion of sound
that threatens to draw me away from my count—

and wait for the player's nod, no beat sacrificed,
our chambered hearts almost synchronized.

Yom Kippur, 2001

To be a Jew is . . . to live when others are dead . . .
—E. Eydoux, translated from the
French by J. Magonet

If I hold fast to these still life frames—
the approaching planes, the towers like gazelles,

necks exposed, fusion of metal, diesel, glass,
the fire ball bloom beyond itself,

implosion, the stunned silence of cells;
if I refuse the sealed certificates of death, refuse

to pick out whole words from ash,
color gray any flash of doubt;

if I give back your love like a gift—
will this chant, this *Kol Nidre*, rise from my lips

like mist, assume the shape of moon or first star,
ghost, shade of Sinai, constant heart?

What Floats Through Me

Under a veil of morphine, I want to look away,
not see the doctor, scrubbed and gloved.
I count each labored step he takes

across the sterile field—thick with risk
like yesterday's raspberry field with thorns
scratching pink each inch of exposed skin.

I chose one berry, so lopsided it collapsed
between my fingertips, its feel imagined
on my tongue, rolled over and over,

every angle examined inside out
like a difficult choice,
until I crushed the cells flat against my thumb—

fingerprint a crimson stain.
I count backward from one hundred,
and feel him reach across blue sheets

for the hypodermic needle—
the saline solution.
The needle buries itself into layers of flesh

as if they were not a part of me,
piercing the final membrane.
I taste salt.

In one dream she floats through me,
riding the curve of my hip like a wave,
as chambers of her defective heart—

like a cave worn down by the sea—
fill and empty in a rhythm
that almost catches hold.

In another dream she is face down
in a riverbed swollen by recent rain,
her tangle of black hair pooled

on the surface like an oil spill.
Her infant gown traps a pocket of air
that keeps her bobbing on each ruffle.

I pull her out, thumping her back,
and wait for breath to sputter and start.
Morning comes, so clear I can follow

its thin string of causality:
events hold their place, explanation
has the solid logic of stone.

Infidelities

Water blue as jay's wings,
but no, not the blue of your eyes—
though stars out of place, yes,
this world's other side,

and glittered strands of pearled beach,
sand ground down fine as silt.
I thought I had all of this fixed
in my script while I floated on my back,

felt your breath coming salty
and ragged as wisps of spume that dissolve
into sheets, sun-blanched
and guanábana white.

The memory of casaba melon is strained,
but I'm sure about the stucco,
walls angled and open,
windows sashed in mauve,

and the conch held to my lips,
its shell wave-smoothed inside out—
the lingering effleurage—
the living part gone.

How could I want that one
pale echo of untanned skin,
thin band fading from your left hand,
one finger from the end? No,

stay where black sepals tongue
the red hibiscus, air perfectly pitched,
yes, and breezes slip a sip of rum—
one part ocean, two parts heat.

Miami Port of Call

Minutes from the Miracle Mile, the Omni Colonnade
surrounds me with detailed attention: room service
at my call and complimentary champagne at my door;
multilingual concierge and chocolate-studded cookies
on a plate.

Yet small comfort in this bi-level suite complete with wet
bar and mahogany armoire, dark as the shadow of
your beard, if no voice mail from you on the dual-line
telephone.

After tomorrow's business tour, the steak au poivre
and carottes juliennes, I'll share a carafe of wine
with my newest confidante—a counselor from Beirut.
She'll ask to see my room, comparing layout, bar, and
bath.

She'll marvel at the marble of my whirlpool, blue veined
and contoured for her hips, and suggest we share a dip.
Tipsy, I'll acquiesce, and we'll turn our backs to shed
our clothes.

I'll hide under jasmine foam, and focus on her hair,
floating on the surface like down. Black as a starling.
Iridescent. I'll tell her how your voice, low and slow,
is as familiar and yet as strange as the shape of her
breasts

sculpted in the bubble bath. How sound carries across a
room. How sound can carry across a thousand miles.
She'll tell me how in the desert, even with her back to
the wind,

sand finds a way into eyes, ears, and even mouth.
I'll show her the times I think of you each day—each
ring of the whorl of my thumb. I'll show her your hand's
brand on my shoulder where you first touched
me—and she'll say yes,

she can feel its heat. Can she smell the raspberry oils?
Can she taste your skin or mouth the feel of you?
I'll save this salve for when she leaves the room, the
turned-down bed,

where I'll synthesize your words. Call me your dancer,
your painted-tongue beauty, your Queen Sophia French
marigold. Let your voice be the last thing I hear before
sleep, playing and replaying, until it becomes so real it
vibrates.

Beekeeper

He could have been a charmer—coaxing snakes
from their bodies to reach for sound
the way plants lean toward the light.

He could have been a keeper—of songs,
notes gathered to shape what was
left unsaid but felt in the rise

and fall of melodic sweep.
Keep back, he warns,
and I wonder how he can hold these bees

barehanded, hoards clinging to his arms,
his fingers barely exposed.
He works the smoker between the super's cracks,

pries off another layer of brood.
The smoke briefly clouds my view
then it lifts beyond the lindens.

I am careful to keep my distance.

La Fonda De San Miguel

Somewhere between his fifth and sixth *caballito,*
blue agave tequila smooth as the Lethe,
when he would talk no more of the Red Sox,

their climb uneven and slow toward first place,
or those Yankees, those spoilers,
or his eldest daughter hiking in Vermont,

and he forgot everything but the ridge
of his left thumb shot with salt,
lick, then clean swig of liquor, suck of lime—

somewhere between there and another drag
on his Havana, another bite of *birria,*
goat meat sweet in maguey leaves,

he offered me a french fry and, leaning close,
his blond hair feathering my cheek, eyelid, lip,
confided that the *empañada* he fed me next

was worth more than all his metaphors,
more than agave growing on volcano slopes,
more than any heart left smoldering home,

even if it was his, even if it wasn't, please,
no moonflowers drooping near ravines,
or wayward blooms in muted citrus tones,

this time let there not be vines or scented trees,
and let the mariachis fade into arches of stone—
no music, no bar, no night.

Making It Up

I can't be sure of my childhood street,
once as familiar as my old room
or the number of houses passed to reach the corner.
The crossing guard's name can't be retrieved, nor the
charm bracelet I gave away
to a friend who moved to the Bronx.
I can't remember if her name was Elsie or Marie,
or if the skirt she wore was white—
its meaning impenetrable.
Was the sky clear or clouded into the shape of a broken
wing? The words exchanged are gone,
but I remember my mother's blame:
Never give away what you can't get back.

Virginity, for instance:
the theme that snaked its way
into my adolescent thoughts—
a stream into which I dangled a line
that might hook something
too big to be dealt with,
or so wriggly it might slip away.
My friends showed off hickies, like trophies,
while I shrank into my turtleneck
and made up back seat stories of double dates,
and fingers that had been around.
I tried on cigar bands and pop-top rings
to see how they suited my left hand
waved in a flourish before a mirror,
and practiced writing *Mrs. Ringo Starr*
in honeymoon-pink pens
bought at the five and dime.

I imagined making it for the first time

in the bed of a Ford pickup truck
with a guy from the Lazy Boy Lounge,
a tattoo on his arm swirled into a heart
holding *Mom.* Or with a hippie
in a waterbed, our bodies stirring up
waves that countered my weight,
that seemed to pull me in,
breaking my concentration to match his breath,
leaving me so breathless and confused
I had to ask if it was over.
Another version placed me
in the bridal suite at the New York Hilton,
netted in white, eyes closed,
gold band on my left fourth finger.
He with matching ring carried me
across the threshold to a bed made up
in white Victorian lace,
mints in gold foil on the pillow—
the version I would save for my daughter.

Posing Nude

It began as a college dare: an art student
tired of flawed peach skins, bananas dangling
over the edge of dark-stained copper bowls,
daylilies languishing in heat.
How many times could he study shadows caught
in crimson folds of cloth draping a stand,
sun angled through an open door?
Better to paint the terrain of breasts exposed
to studio light than to risk groping in the dark
at what lay hidden under layers of wool.

I could not see through the square of canvas
framed by window light, his artist's hand
heard in the tiny *scratch, scratch* of brush strokes,
a bird pecking out of its shell.
I pictured my face a mix of shaded umbers,
a thin pink glaze giving a modest boost
to nose, brow, and chin, and wondered
if a painting could withhold me from myself
the way snapshots are thought to do in Yaqui lore.
I felt my body fill with the scent of oils.

Awaking to Vivaldi's "Four Seasons"

The deer must wonder at this frosted sunrise,
salt lick iced over, each linden limb doubled
in weight, each blade of grass enclosed
in its own sheath that splinters underfoot
beneath a patchwork of Halloween leaves
gathered like souls unearthed and ambered.
Her lover pulls her back under the quilt
and fingers the length of her sternum
as if burnishing a Chinese flute
recovered after nine thousand years,
made from the wing bone of an extinct bird.
"Music of the spheres," he whispers and plays
the sun at middle "G," then Venus,
Mercury, the elements of fire, water, and air
sealed to the end, down to earth,
and still she burns, and she burns, and burns.

Amusia

Another Cape May sunset spreads color
on an ocean sky, each detail not to be missed,
like a coloratura's breath in a difficult passage.

That stroke nearly killed me, she tells me,
a volunteer to push her wheelchair
on wet sand strewn with debris.

It had started as a confusion of keys,
a forgotten combination to open a door.
Lapses, like flickering lights before the dark.

Five years passed, she makes do with what she lacks:
feeling in her left leg and hand, and music.
It's as if the orchestra were submerged.

When she hears the notes swirl low, swishing
like vintage silk, she sways in time,
and her working thumb strokes her wedding band.

Ah, music, she sighs when it's gone,
but was it "La Vie en Rose"
or the Chopin waltz she used to play by heart

against the minute hand of the clock—
fingers scaling the Bösendorfer keyboard
while pedal held and released familiar chords.

Reruns

There's comfort in the way a script plays out
In *Movie Classics* on the late-late show.
The stories ease us back to what is ours.

Curled in flannel wraps or fleece, we count
On certain turns of speech that may evoke
Some comfort in the way a script plays out,

In the way lines fit, hand-me-downs
Conforming to where we want them to go.
The stories ease us back to what is ours.

Bons vivants, endangered flames, and louts
Angle in the camera's neutral hold.
There's comfort in the way a script plays out.

Dietrich riled—a barroom passion doused
By Jimmy Stewart, soon to be her beau.
The stories ease us back to what is ours.

Bacall and Bogart second time around
Survive the vagaries of plot to show
There's comfort in the way a script plays out.
The stories ease us back to what is ours.

Ask Anyone

Ask anyone who's ever lived alone
How houses seem to shift when winter comes.
It's hard to settle in against the cold.

Minor sounds are amplified: groans
From sinking eaves, surfaces that rub.
Anyone who's lived alone knows

The shape silence takes, framed by closing
Doors and intermittent furnace hum.
It's hard to settle in. Against the cold

Bedroom window, nightly rhythms unfold:
A loose screen flaps outside, a broken shutter,
And anyone who's ever lived alone

Knows anything can hide in the quiet approach—
A brush of wings or snowdrifts piling up.
It's hard to settle in against the cold

And empty sheets, the pillow that still holds
The wild scent of an abandoned love.
Ask anyone who's ever lived alone—
It's hard to settle in against the cold.

The Gift

I made this panel myself.
If you are reading it I am dead. . .
—Duane Kearns Puryear,
AIDS Memorial Quilt

The light leaves early these days—
late fall—and soon night and day will be
the same. Only weeks ago the trees
had not turned, but in a flash a man can go gray.
I'm banking on a three-by-six-foot plot
of cloth to save me, my name stitched in red.
I push the needle in and out, and the thread
strains to rise, pulled back by the knotted
weight of where it's been, each gathered hour.
A certain softness eases into each edge
smoothed down by the practiced needle's tread.
The comfort of having learned to live without
fades each loss into a well-worn theme—
yet as slow to resolve as my thimbled need.

Shoring up the Heart

New Year's Eve resolves to New Year's Day,
while pizza oils the doubled cardboard lid.
Champagne goes flat and party toys deflate.
An old year still unsettled, and now this
new one heaps on like snow over layers of ice,
and we go on, as if on sure ground.
Today the yearly jump-start of your life—
you'll wade into the frigid bay and douse
yourself chest-deep, the chill of risk by degrees:
a slip below could mean the heart arrests.
You numb up so quickly, you don't feel
the chill to the bone—just weightlessness.
I'll wait with the lookers-on along the shore
until the air and I can make you warm.

Sighting for Life

Early spring and the wrens croon as if in full
season though we've only seen one honeybee
poised on the edge of the hyacinth's frill
near where we threw the pumpkin Halloween.
No trace is left of its decomposed grin,
as if its soul had flown once the crows
gathered in a black shudder had had their fill.
A pair of geese strut near the lake to comb
the shore for crumbs. "They mate for life," I say,
"uncommon in the order of man or birds."
Awkward in their push and pull of gait,
wing and glide their usual means, the first
dives into the water; the other follows suit,
the surface renewed after the scrawl of two's.

Complications of the Heart

I've heard that hearts are not just simple pumps,
but storage sites of energy—rows
of twitching desires, secret romps
muffled in their four-chambered folds.
Each part carries weight—a string quartet
whose practiced rhythms fit the everyday—
and should a section fail or skip a beat
technology can shock the whole awake.
But still no surgery to transplant love,
uprooting it intact to needed space
when one mate loves too little, one too much—
asymmetry that flusters the heart's pace.
If balance over time won't self-correct,
demand cuts off supply and hearts defect.

Glass! Glorious Glass!

At the Renwick Gallery

Let me be your molten glass, any shape
you desire: free blown chalice; champagne flute
whose rim rings perfect "A's;" embellished coupe.
Emerald and gold-leaf Venetian, I'll stain
your lips with "Inventing Fountains of Thor,"
or glaze them red with "Ruby and Rosette."
Fill me with your fire and make me conform
to your breath, writhing in the heat but not
consumed. Make me bloom birds of paradise
or weave me wings of indigo or white—
I'll be bunting or angel drawn from the heart
of flame, rare as ancient fragments of glass
unearthed near Persia. Hold me to the light
and see through me, sheer as a veiled night.

Miriam at the Waterside

At first a leaf the water catches like the wind,
blue Nile, white Nile, and overhead flocks of thrush.
A raft of twigs and leaves, bound tight by weeds,

unbound again by soft and lazy ripples
smaller than a newborn's hands.
In the rush of wings, a shudder weaves the sky,

basket of reeds, nest of grass, blanket blue as Egypt,
infant lulled by flow and lilt of current, bulrush, purl.
Miriam's song, *weave the waters, weave the reeds,*

from darkness will come light, until drifting out of range.
A sea of reeds, a timbrel in hand, and tallith fingers
fringe the skirts and robes, eddying bare ankles—

sing a new song, sing a song composed of salt and
waves—whatever fits an open mouth, an open palm.
Miriam sings the water into stream, the stream to river,

the river to sea, song and sea rising after heavy rain—
how they hold what must be held until they overflow—
how sorrow holds its joy and holds it once again.

Sing manna, sing *mayim,* sing Miriam—
no clepsydra measuring the wilderness—
sing waterfowl, water milfoil, waterbucks,

water's petals above and below the lily's stems
fed on what resides unseen below.
I am the shaft of light that mines your eyes.
I am the line between waking and sleep.
I am the line unthreaded in its thinning pulse
that pulls you from your dreams.

Prophetess

*. . . We now drink from Miriam's cup,
the waters of Miriam's well in the wilderness.*
—Reconstructionist Passover Haggadah

Drink from this cup as if mine,
and though not wine,

be drunk with dance and music,
the many shapes happiness assumes:

timbrel, wind, reed.
Let me well within you

as you await desert blooms,
or lie down in me as in a sea,

and I will cleanse what is not whole,
will hold what I cannot heal.

I am no Elijah's cup
filled with what you cannot touch.

I will be yours, the lip
where rock meets spring.

A native New Yorker, Nancy Naomi Carlson was educated at Queens College. She earned her Ph.D. at the University of Maryland. Her full-length collection of poetry, *Kings Highway*, won the 1997 Writers' Publishing House competition. She also was a winner of *The Ledge 2002* Poetry Awards competition. Featured on *Poetry Daily*, her work has also appeared in *Poet Lore*, *Poetry*, *Prairie Schooner*, *Shenandoah*, *Southern Humanities Review*, *Southern Poetry Review*, *Texas Review*, and elsewhere. She is an editor for Tupelo Press and runs a community writers' group at Barnes and Noble.